THE OMNIPOTENT PRESENCE GOD *of*

Nathan Botley

TRIUMPH
PUBLISHING

P.O. BOX 690168
BRONX, NEW YORK 10469
716-652-7157
WWW.TRIUMPHPUBLISHING.NET

The Omnipotent Presence of God

Published by:
Triumph Publishing,
New York 10469
www.triumphpublishing.net
718–652–7157

Printed in the United States of America
for Worldwide Distribution.

Dedication

I dedicate this book to my father. You loved me unconditionally all my life and brought me into Your kingdom by sacrificing your only Son. Your faithfulness and gentleness towards me are unwavering. You kept me through extremely trying times, all the while fashioning me to become more like You. Many have wondered why I talk to you so much. They have asked, "why don't you celebrate yourself?" Well, my answer is clear. Anything about me worth celebrating is because of You, so why not make it about You. Why do I talk to You so much? Because I fell in love with Your presence. Your voice is soothing and empowering. I find joy in Your presence, and I realized that there is no other relationship on earth comparable to what I have with You. You have blessed me immensely, and you did it openly where all would know that it was You. This woman you gave me was a wife when I found her. Every characteristic of Esther is found in her. You masterfully orchestrated and weaved our lives into one. There is none like You. So, I dedicate this book, inspired by Your Spirit, to You. I love You, Father.

Left blank intentionally.

Contents

Left blank intentionally.

THE
OMNIPOTENT
PRESENCE
G*O*D

Introduction

There is often talk of how "powerful" and "epic" services are when the saints of God gather. No matter how many times I hear these statements, I am always left trying to define that one word, "Powerful." I am amazed that if this word is defined by what is seen with the natural eye, running, jumping, shouting, I might conclude having many meanings. However, suppose I were to attempt to define the word "powerful" through my spiritual eyes. It is possible that I would come up empty. When referencing the church, powerful or power cannot clearly be defined without considering the Omnipotent God. As the church, we will often minimize a move of God into a highly theatrical display of emotions, which feeds the soul but leaves the spirit starving. Is it possible for the church to experience the God of the bible, who does the unexplainable? Jeremiah said, "Ah, Lord God! Thou have made the heaven and the earth by Thy great power and by Thy outstretched arm! Nothing is too difficult for thee." Jeremiah 32:17 KJV.

Have you ever wondered why our God, Who created the heavens and the earth in a powerful and mind-blowing fashion, would show up in us today, only to make us run, jump and shout? I believe God desires to manifest in His people, the church, just as He did in the former days. He is transforming not only our lives but every person that we encounter. This type of power can only come from the Holy Spirit. It states in Acts 1:8, "But you shall receive power, after that the Holy Spirit has come upon you...." KJV. This verse declares explicitly that this "Power" is inherent in the Holy Spirit and solely in His Domain. The church desperately needs an authentic presence of the Holy Spirit. With the intent to replicate the last great move of God experience, manufacturing services is simply unacceptable.

Let us be clear; the believer is the church. Furthermore, when that believer becomes filled with the Holy Spirit, we will begin to see God's true agenda invade the church and the earth with power. For centuries, we have welcomed God and Jesus, and now I urge you in my writings to send an invitation to the Holy Spirit. I assure you, He Will Accept!

1

THE OMNIPOTENT PRESENCE *of* GOD

Identifying the Church

There are times when we refer to the church as the believer and times when we refer to her as the meeting place. It is essential to know that the church is the Body of Believers, purchased with the shed blood of Jesus Christ, Who is the Head of the church.

"And has put all things under His feet and gave Him to be the Head over all things to the church, which is His Body, the fulness of Him that fills all in all" Ephesians 1:22-23 KJV

We see one of two passages in scripture that tell us that the church belongs to Christ. He fulfills the destiny for which man was created. Christ is the absolute, ultimate authority because of what the cross has accomplished. The church now has its source of life in Him, sustained and directed by His Omnipotence, and is the instrument in which He works. "The fulness of Him that fills all." After considering all who Christ is, the modern-day church is desperately lacking in humility. It is distinctly stated in Acts 17:28 KJV, "For in Him we live, move, and have our being...." The church will not exemplify power or exist at all, for that matter, if authority is not surrendered to Him.

While Jesus was on the coast of Caesarea Philippi, He speaks to Peter, saying, "You are Peter, and upon this rock, I will build My church, and the gates of hell shall not prevail against it" (Matt. 16:18 KJV). The Lord changed his name from Simon Peter to Peter, "a fragment of a rock." But why, Peter, why not one of the other disciples. Because Peter knew Him intimately as the Christ, the Son of the living God, mere human ingenuity did not reveal this to him. Jesus knew that Peter's spiritual knowledge of who He was came only through revelation from the Father. So, upon this immovable mass, Jesus builds His church. He alone is the living rock on which the redeemed [the church] as living stones are built.

For this cause, ownership needed to be established before we moved forward. To perceive that the church belongs to a pastor or its leadership is horribly misleading. With phrases such as "My church" being irresponsibly spoken from podiums and in public arenas, it is understandable why one might believe. This small word, "My," can be detrimental to a leader who has not committed to walking in the Spirit. Though small, this two-letter word denotes possession. If not careful and pride enters in, fulfilling the lust of the flesh is imminent.

Now, let us look at the second scripture.

"And He is the Head of the Body, the church...." Colossians 1:18

The text emphasizes the leadership of Jesus Christ and His Omnipotent power. Christ is Head simply because He holds all things together and that He is Savior of a lost and dying world. The implications of this teaching are profound. First, pastors and church leaders are to surrender ultimate leadership and authority to the Lord Jesus Christ. He alone determines the destiny of the church.

For this reason, shepherds need to hear and know the voice of the Lord if they are to feed the sheep with knowledge and understanding (Jer. 3:15). In turn, the church follows Christ first and earthly leaders second, as those leaders emulate Christ. Paul says, "Be imitators of me, as I am of Christ" (I Corinthians 11:1 KJV).

Many people today believe that the church is the place where they attend on Sundays. This belief, in no way, defines the biblical understanding of the church. The word "church" is a translation of the Greek word "ekklesia," defined as "an assembly" or "called-out ones." The original meaning of *church* is not implying a building or erected structure, but people. Typically, when you ask someone about the church, they will give you a name and location. However, this response is not at all accurate.

"Likewise greet the church that is in their house...." Romans 16:5 KJV

Paul speaks to the Body of Believers that are in the building, not the building itself. Knowing our identity as the church is critical. Why? Because significant amounts of money and effort are put into designing and erecting buildings with false beliefs that that is what you call "a church." I often wondered how mature the "true church" would be in these modern times if we exchanged our hammers for bibles. Isn't it amazing that God calls pastors to build the church, and pastors call carpenters to build a church? I am not at all implying that a meeting place is not essential. However, I believe that the church's identity becomes smeared when divine purpose collides with an ulterior motive.

The word purpose is defined as the reason for which something is done or created. The Apostle Paul states, "Know you not that you [the church] are the temple of God and that the Spirit of God dwells in you" (1 Cor. 3:16-17 KJV). One of our purposes as the called-out church is to be carriers of the Spirit of God. Paul talks of a temple that's not only splendid in appearance but "Holy" because of His presence. We will discuss God's presence later, but I will say this, how can we be a powerful temple [church] of God if God is not present. Could it be that, because of carnal desires, we are trying to keep the world as our landlords rather than turning ownership over to the One Who holds the deed?

We are the temple of God and with great purpose. That purpose is to make disciples of Jesus Christ. He is the image of God; we are the image of Christ. We, in Christ Jesus, received the adoption as sons, a relationship with the Father. He is the Light of the world. He, in us, makes us lights unto the world also. The church has the responsibility of carrying the Holy Spirit throughout the earth. The world needs to see God in us, not merely us. Our words and our actions should reflect the character and attributes of the Father who lives in us. Verse Seventeen says, "If any man defiles [desecrate or violate] the Temple of God, he shall God destroy. For the Temple of God is Holy, which temple are you?" Our physical bodies must be a living sacrifice unto God. Meaning, we must stay Holy by ever making the cross the object of our faith. To fail to the prescribed purpose for our lives opens us up to Satan's devices. We are "Holy" by virtue of being in Christ Jesus. We remain "Holy" by acknowledging that when Christ died, we died with Him. When He was resurrected, we were as well.

"I am crucified with Christ; nevertheless, I live, yet not I, but Christ lives in me. And the life which I now live in the flesh, I live by the faith of the Son of God who loved me and gave Himself for me." Galatians 2:20 KJV

As the foundation of all victory, Paul reminds us that it is not by our strength and ability but by virtue of dying with Him and being raised with Him in the newness of life. We will never fully understand who we are until we know and receive what He did for us. It is not enough for us to only know that "He got up with all power in His hand." Acknowledging the fact that the resurrection of Jesus Christ was the beginning of the church. He ascended back to heaven and is seated with God. Moreover, He, the Holy Spirit, descended and is seated in us, the powerful church.

Sonship and the Church

The times that we are in are indeed perilous. Stress and fear are increasing daily, affecting even the identity and character of many. However, should this be, as people who proclaim to "Know Him?"

"Thou wilt keep him in perfect peace, whose mind is stayed on Thee; because he trusted in Thee." Isaiah 26:3 KJV

I find it interesting that some try to keep their mind focused on a God they do not truly trust. I know this is somewhat harsh, but because scripture is true, the mind that remains on God, He keeps in perfect peace. This leads me to my point; being the church is knowing that you belong to God and have a relationship with Him. It is exceptionally difficult to trust someone that you do not know.

Times of vast technology use has put a tremendous strain on relationships. There is little face-to-face interaction, mostly texting and messaging, making it difficult to have a real relationship with someone. Some would rather send God a text because they do not have "time" to spend with Him face-to-face. As children of God, we were created for a relationship with Him.

"He predestinated us to adoption as children [sonship] by Jesus Christ to Himself, according to the good pleasure of His will." Ephesians 1:5 KJV

God chose in advance for us to become His children. He chose in the act of love and as part of His divine plan. "Predestined" is from a word meaning "to mark out beforehand." This word has two parts: *before* and *to mark out the boundaries or limits*. The idea is that God, beforehand, determined our destiny and put limits on it.

The word predestined is always referred to as an action by God. It was an act of God and Him alone to choose us. He marked out from eternity past that He would adopt believers as sons through Jesus Christ's redeeming blood. His motivation came from Himself. Knowing this should seal our identity in Him. When man rejects you, remain still because it was God who chose you.

He chose you "for His good pleasure," and it was His will to do so. God's will is the rule of His actions and all His acts of Grace and goodness towards his people. We should never lose the fact of our identity.

We understand that sonship is being adopted by the Father, but what makes us "sons?"

"For as many as are led by the Spirit of God, they are the sons of God." Romans 8:14

The word "son" is not gender-related. It describes a church that follows the leadership of its Father. As natural sons and daughters look to their earthly fathers for protection, guidance, and direction, we, even more so, should look to our heavenly Father for the same. He desires to father us. However, we must turn everything over and follow Him.

One of the most remarkable experiences in my walk with Christ is learning to be led by the Holy Spirit. The world encourages you to "just do you" and "be your own boss." However, this is poor advice when trying to follow God. We have not been created so He could join our work, but that we would join His. The Apostle Paul tells us in Ephesians 2:10, "For we are His workmanship, created in Christ Jesus unto good works, which God has before ordained that we should walk in them." As sons of God, if we are His workmanship, our salvation cannot be of ourselves. We are saved by His Grace and are now being led by His Spirit. Therefore, we should no longer be following the desires of our flesh. If the sin nature is dominating our lives, we are certainly not living as sons.

Being led by the Spirit of God consists of being baptized by the Spirit. I remember the senior saints would love to say, "I am saved, sanctified, and filled with the Holy Ghost!" In modern-day church gatherings, this is rarely echoed, mostly because teachings on the Holy Spirit have been replaced with membership growth tactics and retention meetings. Imagine if more books were written, seminars held, training sessions organized, videos produced on being baptized in the Holy Spirit? Your sonship [adoption as sons] is undeniably necessary. However, may I expound the way of the Lord more perfectly?

"And a certain Jew named Apollos, born at Alexandria, an eloquent man, and mighty in the scriptures came to Ephesus. This man was instructed in the way of the Lord, and being fervent in the spirit, he spoke and taught the things of the Lord diligently, knowing only the baptism of John. And he began to speak boldly in the synagogue; when Aquila and Priscilla had heard, they took him unto them, and expounded unto him the way of God more perfectly." Acts 18:24-26 KJV

Apollos was a man whom Paul esteemed greatly. He was persuasive in speaking the word of God. However, he only knew the baptism of John, which was salvation and water baptism. His knowledge was significantly limited, respecting Grace and the baptism of the Holy Spirit. Teaching boldly in the synagogue, he was heard and approached by Aquila and Priscilla, Paul's followers. They instructed him to the full complement of salvation by the Grace of God exclusively, correct water baptism, and the baptism of the Holy Spirit with evidence of speaking with new tongues. Now, advanced in his understanding, Apollos had become more proficient in this most excellent message of the Grace of God that comes through sonship. He was able to teach efficiently on salvation and the necessity of being filled with the Holy Spirit.

Natural sons possess their father's DNA. This DNA presents the fundamental and distinctive characteristics or qualities of the father that manifests in the son. When the father and son share the same DNA, the relationship cannot be questioned. Likewise, for the sons [remember, not gender related] of God, if He is our Father, then there is an unquestionable match in our DNA. Our character is the sum of our disposition, thoughts, intentions, desires, and actions that reflect His image.

"So, God created mankind in His own image; in the image of God, he created them; male and female, he created them." Genesis 1:27

The church should be a representation of God in the earth. A church adopted, set apart, and follows the Holy Spirit's leading will reflect the Father's image. What the world need is for the sons of God to take their rightful position in the Kingdom of God. If our identity continues to waver, this world will never come to the knowledge of the Truth. We are God's Glory carriers. His Glory is that which emanates from His character that's a part of us. In the realm of the Spirit, I sense a church confident in whom she is—having the resemblance of a mighty warrior who blows the trumpet when danger is seen. She gathers those that are wounded to heal, teach, empower, and direct them. I see a church that has become aggressive in finding the lost, leading them to the Father, and destroying the strongholds in their lives. This Glorious church is bold in speech, wise in approach, yet settled in identity. I hear her shouting and proclaiming throughout the earth, "For the Spirit of the Lord God is upon me; because the Lord hath anointed me to preach good tidings unto the meek; he hath sent me to bind up the brokenhearted, to proclaim liberty to the captives, and the openings of the prison to them that are bound" (Is. 61:1 KJV). Glory! To the Most High God, Your church Lord embraces her Identity.

2

THE
OMNIPOTENT
PRESENCE
G*of*OD

Embracing the Presence of God

If you were to ask random people today, "Are you a part of a Holy Spirit-filled gathering of believers?" Many would answer with a resounding, "yes." Furthermore, if you would also ask, "how do you know that the Spirit of God is present?" They would respond by saying, "well, we have good singing, shouting, dancing, and great preaching." Suppose their response is accurate in describing God's presence. If that is the case, something is tremendously wrong if we consistently participate in these services and remain powerless.

I remember the Lord speaking to me sometime during the Fall of 2018, saying, "there are many forms of Godliness, and most lack presence and power." I would be remiss if I heard God and did not self-evaluate. Like many leaders today, we'd never intentionally plan a gathering without first being instructed by the Holy Spirit. However, we can become so indulged in our ideas that we foolishly navigate our way from the will of God. Too often, is this very thing happening. We create the "form of Godliness" but fail to acknowledge Him first. We want Him to "show up" and "move mightily," but should we expect Him? David asked God, "Search me, O God, and know my heart. Try me and know my thoughts. And see if there be any wicked way in me and lead me in the way of everlasting" (Ps. 139: 23-24 KJV). Have we examined our motives? Have we asked God to search our hearts?

"For men shall be lovers of their own selves, covetous, boasters, proud, blasphemers, disobedient to parents, unthankful, unholy. Without natural affection, trucebreakers, false accusers, incontinent, fierce, despisers of those who are good. Traitors, heady, high-minded, lovers of pleasures more than lovers of God." 2 Timothy 3:2-4 KJV

If I might interpose a personal remark here; In no way are my intentions to speak down on the church. My love for God and His people encourages me to point out obstacles in our lives that hinder our ability to embrace His presence. As a watchman, I cannot hear the trumpet and heed not warning the people (Ez. 33:4 KJV). How we present ourselves to God can tremendously affect our personal experience with Him. The character of men described in II Timothy 3:2-4 could do just that.

We want to think that we are exempt from these fleshly traits. And yes, every effort should be given to do so. The church is encouraged to "walk in the Spirit, and you shall not fulfill the lust of the flesh" (Gal. 5:16 KJV). Our instructions are to order our behavior, and we can only do so by placing complete trust in the finished work of Jesus Christ on the cross. The existence of the sin nature is always lurking around the life of the believer. It declares the consciousness of corrupt desires. The only way to maintain Christlike character is to give ourselves entirely to the Holy Spirit, embracing His presence and following His leading.

What is the Presence of God

A Hebrew word for presence is "face" and connotes a personal relationship. It also translates face-to-face. Can you imagine being in a face-to-face relationship with God? Of course, we are speaking figuratively and not literally. However, I often wonder how church gatherings would be if all who attended had a personal relationship with God. I am not at all insinuating similarity in relationship but oneness with the Father. What Love and Presence there would be.

"The Lord, your God, is in your midst, a mighty one who will save; He will rejoice over you with gladness; He will quiet you by His love; He will exult over you with loud singing." Zephaniah 3:17 ESV

Here we see God speaking to Jerusalem, promising that He will reside in this city mightily to prevent evil. Once a rebellious city, Jerusalem will give itself to the One who is in the midst, offering Himself as a Righteous Judge, able to correct its evil. This transformation is an example of what having a face-to-face relationship with God will do for us. It is an invitation for Him to dwell in our midst. Having the authority to correct us, save us, rejoice over us with gladness, quiet us by His love, and exult over us with loud singing. Wow, we can have all of this if we would learn how to embrace His presence.

Shekhinah is another word used. It is the English transliteration of a Hebrew word meaning "dwell or settling" and denotes the dwelling or settling of God's divine presence. Our bodies are the temple of the Holy Spirit (I Cor. 6:19). It is the place where the Spirit of God dwells, the sanctuary of the Holy Spirit. David says, "Where shall I go from Your spirit? Or where shall I flee from Your presence?" (Ps. 139:7 KJV) Because we belong to Him, He is always with us.

"And I heard a great voice out of heaven saying, Behold, the Tabernacle of God is with men, and He will dwell with them, and they shall be His people, and God Himself shall be with them, and be their God." Revelation 21:3

This voice that John heard was the voice of God flowing out of the Throne. The text proclaims that which God intended from the beginning. John has seen the New Heaven and the New Earth. The first heaven and the first earth, referring to the original creation marred by sin, will pass away. We will then become new and one with God because of the complete absence of sin.

I think it is appropriate to give credence to the fact that God is Omnipresent. He not only dwells in us, making it impossible to flee His presence but can also be everywhere at the same time, as though all-enveloping. This fact should heighten our faith. God orders our steps for a destination, walks in us along the way, and is waiting on us upon arrival. If this does not blow your mind, think of this: He desires to be this way with us. In a world filled with rejection, separation, and isolation, our Father truly wants us. Wow, the Love that He shows us is incomprehensible.

In talking about embracing the presence of God, we use a familiar word, "Omnipresence." If not properly understood, this word could have a person believe that their carnal will is God's will. Might I add this, just because God is everywhere [omnipresent] does not imply that He is in [supports] everything?

"The eyes of the Lord are in every place, beholding the evil and the good." Proverbs 15:3 KJV

What is portrayed in this Proverb is that God's all-presence brings man under great observation. Such constant observation is unsettling to the carnal heart. Still, to the Spirit-filled heart who embraces His presence, such knowledge invigorates the spirit and comforts the soul. I often hear worldly organizations such as cults or groups that practice exclusivity claim that their functions and beliefs are biblically foundational. My heart breaks because misinterpretation of scripture, or more so, the lack of spiritual revelation, causes one to believe that God is in the function. Yes, God is there. However, He is not in it. His eyes are present, beholding the evil and the good.

"Can any hide himself in secret places that I shall not see him? Saith the Lord. Do not I fill Heaven and Earth? Saith the Lord." Jeremiah 23:24 KJV

The Presence of God carries a wide range of meanings. In the Garden of Eden, His presence brought fear to Adam and Eve after their fall (Gen. 3:8). False gods became powerless in His presence (Is. 19:1). God's presence brought comfort to Joshua (Josh. 1:5), deliverance to David (I Samuel 17:37), and nearness in worship through the Bread of the Presence (2 Chron. 4:19), to name a few. Although God's presence is everywhere, remember this, God's Spirit lives in those of us who believe. John 14:23 says, "Jesus answered him, If anyone loves me, he will keep my word, and my Father will love him and will come to him and make our home with him." I am humbled in knowing that God the Father, Jesus Christ, and the Holy Spirit live in the heart of the one who believes. In other words, you are a carrier of Presence!

The Danger in Mishandling the Presence of God

The responsibility of properly handling the presence of God falls on the shoulders of the believer. However, this is not to say that we have control of or dictate what God does. The implication has to do with reverencing Him. We cannot lose sight of the fact that "we are" because "He is." No matter the depth of our anointing, we are still subjected to the sovereignty of His Presence.

"And every creature which is in heaven, and on the earth, and under the earth, and such as are in the sea, and all that are in them, heard I saying Blessing, and honor, and glory, and power, be unto Him that sits upon the throne, and unto the Lamb forever and ever." Revelation 5:13 KJV

By hearing, John testifies to Christ's death as atonement being the basis of the restoration of all things. The actions of Jesus at the cross guaranteed complete victory over Satan and all of darkness, which will, in the coming age, cleanse Heaven and earth in totality and forever. Because of this great testimony, the saints' hearts should become that of the living creatures who give honor and thanks to Him Who sits on the Throne (Rev. 4:9). If these creatures continuously honor, glorify, and be thankful in the Presence of God, how can we who have known the glorious redemption of our Lord Jesus Christ do any less? Constantly remembering that He is Father, and we are His children can solidify a proper relationship with Him. When this is lost, our reverence for His presence becomes jeopardized. We then fall prey to self-will or personal agenda.

So, if the believer is responsible for properly handling the presence of God, what is the fundamental truth that serves as the foundation of our behaviors. We will begin with the appointment of the Levites.

"But you shall appoint the Levites over the Tabernacle of Testimony, and over all the vessels thereof, and over all things that belong to it: they shall bear the Tabernacle, and all the vessels thereof; and they shall minister unto it, and shall encamp round about the Tabernacle. (51) And when the Tabernacle sets forward, the Levites shall take it down: and when the Tabernacle is pitched, the Levites shall set it up: and the stranger that comes near shall be put to death." Numbers 1:50-51

In the study of God's presence, may I give a disclaimer about the Levites' responsibilities? In no way am I claiming complete understanding. I believe that scripture provides us with enough information to conclude that Presence requires reverence, as instructed and demonstrated by the Levites. I desire that we learn to acknowledge and be more respectful to God and His

Presence! Our reverence of the Father is not how well we can move a crowd, but can we move the heart of God by highly esteeming Him?

In the book of Exodus 31:18, we see God giving Moses the Ten Commandments, also known as the "tables of testimony." The ark which contained these tables was called the "ark of testimony" (Ex. 25:22). The tabernacle in which the ark was placed was called the "tabernacle of testimony" (Ex. 38:21). The tabernacle was the tent pitched by the Levites, which covered the ark of the testimony. The word testimony refers to the conditional agreement made between God and the children of Israel at the Mount of Sinai. The Tabernacle of Testimony was where God's glory dwelt amongst His people and the responsibility of the chosen Levites to bear it along with every vessel it contained.

While the Tabernacle of Testimony was very important, the Ark of Testimony bears the same. Again, it contained the Ten Commandments, and no one could touch the ark but the high Priest.

"And when Aaron and his sons have made an end of covering the sanctuary, and all the Vessels of the Sanctuary, as the camp is to set forward; after that, the sons of Kohath shall come to bear it: but they shall not touch any holy thing, lest they die...." Numbers 4:15

What? Mishandling the Presence of God can lead to death? This very thing is exemplified in I Chronicles 13:1-10. While carrying the Ark of Testimony, the oxen pulling the cart stumbles. A man named Uzzah puts forth his hand on the ark to stabilize it, and God struck him, and he died. Before we become troubled in our spirit, let us look at the events that led to this. In verse one, it reads, "And David consulted with captains of thousands and hundreds, and with every leader." In bringing the Ark of Testimony to Jerusalem, David consulted with men. It does not say that he consulted with God. Great danger lies in the consultation of man's wisdom when orders by God have already been established. The excitement of sharing an idea with others often shackles us to their opinion, and if heeded, disaster is imminent.

David fell prey to this, thus deciding to carry the ark on a "new cart" (2 Sam. 6:3). The Law of Moses said that the children of the Levites must carry the Ark upon their shoulders (I Chron. 15:15). These men, also known as Priest, were representative examples of Christ. Nevertheless, Israel borrowed the Philistines' way and carried the Ark, contrary to God's Word, on a "new cart." Doing this resulted in the death of Uzzah. In this act of God, He showed and taught His people about His holiness and their unworthiness. He demonstrated to them that His commands were not suggestions to be negotiated with the wisdom of man. He wanted to teach them that they must become obedient in all things, whether they understood His reason or not.

The Ark of Testimony represented the Presence of God with His people and had to be handled properly. Now because of the death, burial, and resurrection of Jesus, that Presence resides in us.

"So we have come to know and to believe the love that God has for us. God is love, and whoever abides in love abides in God, and God in him." 1 John 4:16 ESV

Praise God that we no longer have to carry an Ark on our shoulders. Inside of every person that loves God and keeps His Word, there is Presence. Our responsibility to Him is to maintain a holy and righteous vessel. Yes, He lives in us. However, we still must carry Him properly. The Bible says in I Corinthians 3:16-17 KJV, "Know you not that you are the Temple of God and that the Spirit of God dwells in You? If any man defiles the temple of God, he shall God destroy. For the Temple of God is Holy, which Temple are you?" Can we answer this question today? Whether we acknowledge it or not, it is always about what He wants, and His Presence is to be revered.

Embracing Him and His Word

Embrace means accepting or supporting willingly and enthusiastically; holding closely as a sign of affection. Embracing God is closely related to loving Him. Those of us who spend personal time in worship understand what it means to embrace His Presence. There is no other relationship on earth that compares to having a relationship with God. The oneness and intimacy that come from loving and embracing Him are unexplainable. The Great Commandment says, "And you shall love the Lord your God, with all your heart, and with all your soul, and with all your might" (Duet. 6:5). My question is, are we enthusiastic about doing so? Is spending time with Him and not asking for anything difficult? Do you become agitated in prolonged worship services when others are lying before Him? If so, ask God to examine your heart.

"Examine me, O Lord, and prove me, try my reins and my heart."
Psalms 26:2

Because there is a constant battle within us between flesh and spirit (Gal. 6:17), we need God always to test our motives. Our motive is a massive hindrance when attempting to embrace God's Presence. Every child of God should inquire of the Holy Spirit to probe deep within the heart to "prove me" and see if our relationship with Him is healthy and not motivated by wrong motives. The idea that we are perfect and that God is pleased with all that we do is preposterous. I have seen worship services that have become heavily saturated with God's presence countless times, brought to a halt because someone grabs the microphone who struggles with pride. He will not allow any flesh [human effort] to glory in His Presence (I Cor. 1:29). The Grace of God, which enables us to come freely into His presence, is humbling, realizing that that was not possible before the cross. Many will say, "it is not about quantity, it is about quality," as it pertains to spending time with Him. Well, the more time I spent with Him, the more I desired to be with Him. I have learned that the quantity of time greatly impacted that time's quality, which taught me how to be patient in the moment and embrace His Presence. Remember, God wants to be wanted! Besides, it is almost impossible to embrace someone when you would rather be elsewhere.

Throughout our journey as believers, the visible actions of wanting things our way drastically increase. Direct instruction from the Word of God is falsely interpreted to justify personal desires garnished with self-centeredness. Is it possible to embrace God's presence that submits to His Word if we do not

The Omnipotent Presence of God

acknowledge His Word as infallible? David says, "…for You have magnified Your Word above Your name" (Ps. 138:2b KJV). God's Word is His promise to His church that He highly extols above His Reputation and Character for faithfulness and goodness. Therefore, it is foolish to think that we can enthusiastically embrace His Presence while consciously altering His Word. The impulse to do things my way and submission to that urge indicates an improper alignment in my relationship with the Father. How I relate to Him must not come from a mindset that God's responsibility is to bring to pass all that I desire with blessing following. So, what am I saying? We must become obedient lovers of His Word before we can appreciate and embrace His Presence.

30

3

THE OMNIPOTENT PRESENCE of GOD

Seeking the Heart and Will of the Father

Upon receiving instructions from God to write this chapter, I had to ask, as the church who are carriers of His Presence, are we interested in the Will of the Father? Please give me some grace as you read. I must bring to light certain actions the church took, who will claim, "this is God's Will." We are often deceived into believing that "our will" is "God's Will." It is possible when we mature in Him, and we have become submitted vessels. However, in perilous times and situations, I see time after time decisions being made, and actions are taken with no biblical foundation or support. I used to believe that "as smart as I thought I was," what I was doing was what God wanted me to do merely because it was good works. It was not until I came into the realization that, "I have been crucified with Christ, it is no longer I who live, but Christ lives in me, and the life which I now live in the flesh I live by faith in the Son of God, Who loved me and gave Himself for me" (Gal.2:20 NKJV). What I am skilled to do may not necessarily be what I have been created to do, and what I want to do, I can't because I no longer belong to myself. If He loves me and gave Himself for me, it behooves me to seek His heart and Will for my life. I was advised four years ago to "follow the leading of the Lord." That advice proved to be life-altering. When following God in an attempt to know His heart, hearing His Voice is necessary!

Hearing God

Jesus was in constant communion with the Father. In John 5:30 (KJV), He says, "I can of Mine Own Self do nothing. As I hear, I judge, and My judgement is Just because I seek not Mine Own Will, but the Will of the Father which has sent Me." Jesus, in His Humanity, received all authority from the Father. Unlike many today, before He acted (judged), He heard. One of the most significant requirements in seeking the heart and Will of the Father is having an ability and desire to hear. His judgement was not Just because He was Jesus; it was Just because it came from the Father. He, as His Self, could do "nothing." He did what He heard, not what He felt. Why, because he sought the Heart of the Father. In this verse, what is revealed to us is that the human consciousness of the Son became the basis for the Father's judgement. An absolute Word was released through the human lips of Jesus, accomplishing the Will of God. As the obedient Son, Jesus was given the tongue of the learned.

"The Lord God [the Father] has given Me [Jesus] the tongue of the learned, that I should know how to speak a Word in season to him who is weary. He wakens morning by morning. He wakens My ear to hear as the learned" Isaiah 50:4 KJV

The intent of the Holy Spirit in this verse portrays the inexhaustible Power of God that chose to send His Obedient Son to the cross to redeem not only Israel but the entire world. The tongue of the learned depicts Jesus as having the ability to speak words given to Him by the Father in the proper season. A popular phrase in today's church is "the Lord told me to tell you." And after hearing "what the Lord told them to tell me," I am left discerning, was this the Lord? If so, for what season? Jesus said that the father awakened His ear to hear as the learned. God held immediate and constant communication with His Son. It was not like it was with the old testament prophets where He occasionally spoke to them. In the present time, because of what took place at Calvary, we have the Person of the Holy Spirit living inside Who speaks to our spirit, the Will of God. All of what was exemplified by Jesus was not for His benefit, but rather that "He should know how to speak a Word in season to them who are weary." Ask God today to awaken your ear to hear as the learned.

"But if from thence you shall seek the Lord, your God, you shall find Him, if you seek for Him with all your heart and with all your soul" Deuteronomy 4:29

"And you shall seek Me, and find Me when you shall search for Me with all your heart" Jeremiah 29:13

My dad would often say to me, "Nathan, you need to learn to listen." He would notice that I would stare at him while he spoke, but when sent off with instruction, I had no idea what he said because I had not yet learned to listen. I frequently found myself returning to my father, asking him to repeat himself, which he did not like. As I grew into adulthood and as a believer, my heavenly Father had to teach me what my natural father attempted to do so many times. I have now learned the essentials in listening to and hearing the Voice of God. God is found when He is sought after with diligence. Irrespective of what you did or did not do, if you seek Him with all your heart and soul, you will find Him.

One of the most asked questions today is, "how do I hear from God?" At some point, we have all asked this question. It is common because we all want to know what God has planned for us. The bible answers this in Hebrews 1:1-2 (KJV), which says, "God, Who at sundry times and in divers manners, spoke in times past unto the fathers by the Prophets. (2) Has in these last days spoken to us by His Son Whom He has appointed Heir of all things, by Whom also He made the worlds." Previously, God spoke through Holy men [Prophets] as they were moved by the Holy Spirit (II Pet.1:21), as He still does today. However, because of the dispensation of Grace, which is the church age, we can now hear God from a voice that is now within us, Jesus. We must not neglect to seek after God. When we seek, we are attempting to find. The more you seek Him, the more you desire to do so. As the desire grows, your relationship with Him grows as well. Now you have faith because you heard His Voice (Rom. 10:17).

I Can Hear, Now What?

Let us return to a previous statement made by Jesus in John 5:30, "I can of Mine Own Self do nothing, as I hear, I Judge...." Jesus' action (judgment) was that of the Obedient Servant. You ask, "now what?" Well, it is simple. Be obedient to what He said. The Will of God will never be known by the person who is disobedient.

Instructions are given to believers pertaining to the Will of the Father.

"I beseech you, therefore, brethren, by the mercies of God, that you present your bodies a Living Sacrifice, holy, acceptable unto God, which is your reasonable service. (2) And be not conformed to this world but be ye transformed by the renewing of your mind, that you may prove that what is that good, and acceptable, and perfect Will of God." Romans 12:1-2 KJV

While writing this book, our world is amid a pandemic. Many believers, including church leadership, are asking the question, "what is God saying? What is He doing?" If these verses were examined and revelation was asked for, there would not have been such a vast number of opinions. In the text, Paul speaks pointedly about consecration. Consecration had become a "religious activity" to the church and not a lifestyle. Therefore, he encourages the Romans to live a holy and righteous life. This lifestyle could not have been accomplished without their total acceptance of the finished work of Jesus Christ on the cross. Paul stresses that a holy physical body, i.e., "temple," is all that is acceptable to God. One of the most significant deficits in the modern-day church is the standard of Holy

Living. It is rarely spoken of or preached. Why? I found present a spirit of fear that attacks church leaders and hinders them from speaking on things like "living a consecrated and holy life." This villain [an evil spirit of fear] has been allowed to deceive many of their spiritual authority. Evidence of this is apparent during this pandemic. As pastors, we have mastered growing the church in numbers but failed at growing them in knowledge and understanding of the Word of God. When we should be set apart and noticed by the world as a light that cannot be hidden, reflecting God's character, there is little difference to be noticed.

Therefore, Paul instructs them not to be similar to the world, having its ways or conversation. Here lies the definition of consecration, set apart and declared sacred for God's purpose and will. Is there a noticeable difference between you and the world? Do you still have a desire for sin? Do you indulge in enjoyable recollection of past sinful events from the "good ole days?" If so, these are the ways of the world and are direct hindrances to knowing His will. Ask God to strip off those sins that so easily entangle you (Heb. 12:1 NIV). Paul encourages them to change their thinking. They were in dire need of transformed minds.

You cannot obtain spiritual results through carnal thinking. I have heard from many saints, "well, God gives us common sense." This is true, but to be used with practical matters. Common sense loses its effectiveness when that which is common can no longer be sensed. In other words, common sense, even though given to us by God, has limitations. Our perception of a thing is formed by what we sense through seeing, hearing, tasting, feeling, or smelling. Our perception is where we will find "our will." Once again, all given to us by God. However, if not careful, we will begin to lean to our understanding and not acknowledge Him. To know [discern] the good and acceptable and perfect Will of God, we must give our life for His purpose. We must live holy, no longer conform to the world, and start thinking spiritually. This is what the Holy Spirit is trying to bring forth in our lives.

Obedience

Now that we have heard the Word of God, let us become obedient. Scripture has much to say about the believer and obedience. Obedience is necessary if we are going to live as people consecrated to the Father. Jesus exemplified such obedience unto death.

"And being found in fashion as a man, He humbled Himself and became obedient unto death, even the death of the Cross." Philippians 2:8

The character of the Son of Man in His death presents disgrace and degradation. All of which was necessary to redeem humanity. Through it all, He willingly brought Himself under the authority of His Father and subjected Himself to death. Jesus says to His disciples, "If any man will come after Me, let him deny himself, and take up his cross and follow Me" (Matt. 16:24 KJV). He gave those instructions to His students because He knew the importance of self-denial. Denying ourselves, obeying; these words are exceedingly difficult for some believers to hear. Some believe it is a sign of weakness, or you tell me I cannot do what I want. Obedience to the Father in all things gives a fulfilling life and shows our love for Him. The Words of Jesus, "If you love Me, keep My commandment" (Jn. 14:15 KJV). Any believer who refuses to obey the command of God can rightly be asked, "Why do you call me Lord, Lord and do not do what I say?" (Lk. 6:45 ESV)

Obedience is defined as "dutiful or submissive compliance to the Word of God." Dutiful means it is our reasonable service and our obligation to obey God. Jesus remained obedient to His Father by giving His life for us. When we have become submissive, there is an indication that we have yielded our wills to God. We also understand that when the Father speaks, these are not merely suggestions but commands of scripture. He clearly delineates His Instructions. The One in authority is God, whose authority is unequivocal and complete. As believers, our focus should be to comply totally with all that God has commanded. If we cannot do this, then the question must be asked again, "Why do you call Me Lord, Lord, and do not do what I say?"

"Not everyone who says unto Me, Lord, Lord, shall enter the Kingdom of Heaven; but he who does the Will of My Father which is in Heaven." Matthew 7:21 KJV

The repetition of the word "Lord" expresses astonishment as if to say, "are we to be disowned?" Obedience to the Father relieves us from the fear of being left behind. At times, God's commands appear trying, but with the help that comes from the Holy Spirit, we do not have to be enslaved to fleshly desires. It is heartbreaking to witness how masterfully the modern-day church has become in finding scripture to justify sin and disobedience. The phrase "you can't judge me" seemingly has become a shield that is lifted to protect carnal sheep from scriptural correction. All the while, doing "ministry" with the appearance of holiness and righteousness and never properly coming under the authority of God-ordained leadership. Obedience to the Father is not suggestive to the believer. Sincere love for God is keeping His Commandments (Jn. 14:15). The word "commandment" in its primary and most straightforward form is a rule or charge given by the Father through His Word that must be kept.

For a long time, I have watched people walk in what we call "a heavy anointing." I have noticed an extreme difference between their lives and the lives of the average churchgoer. There were a few personal convictions that they had that allowed them to become one with God. However, one of those convictions stood out more than others. They constantly sought the Heart and Will of their heavenly Father. Seeking the heart of the Father undoubtedly comes at a price because never is that person following popular opinion. They often have to forsake loved ones and family for the Will of God. Seeking the Heart and Will of the Father takes determination and has to be intentional. The temptation of saying and doing things our way is always present. Why? Because we all have an opinion. It takes dedication in your relationship with Him to drive you to please Him. Seeking God's Will undoubtedly will never satisfy our natural man. Still, it will grant the Holy Spirit liberty to carry out the Father's plans for us.

"Now the God of Peace, that brought again from the dead our Lord Jesus, that Great Shepherd of the sheep, through the Blood of

the Everlasting Covenant, (21) Make you perfect in every good work to do His Will, working in you that which is well-pleasing in His sight, through Jesus Christ; to Whom be Glory forever and ever." Amen. Hebrews 13:20-21 KJV

4

THE OMNIPOTENT PRESENCE of GOD

No Compromise

"Joyful are the people of integrity, who follow the instructions of the Lord. (2) Joyful are those who obey his laws and search for him with all their hearts. (3) They do not compromise with evil, and they walk only in His paths. (4) You have charged us to keep your commandments carefully." Psalms 119:1-4 NLT

Many obstacles should caution the church. If these are unnoticed, they can become land mines in our relationship with the Father. To make concessions or accommodations for someone who disagrees with the Word of God is to compromise. The Bible is clear that our heavenly Father does not condone compromising His standards. As I have said numerous times before, the Bible is not a book of suggestions given to us to decide whether or not we agree. It is the infallible Word of God that brings joy to those who obey. In this world, there are many clichés, doctrines, and aphorisms. The church cannot risk replacing the Word of God with these. Unfortunately, some endeavor to make "catchy phrases" part of their biblical discussions that's sure to get you a dramatic response but contains little-to-no spiritual sustenance. The Bible is the inspired Word of God (2 Tim. 3:16). It did not come from man's intellect, nor was it left to man's critical explanation or interpretation of the text. It is God-breathed, and Holy Spirit revealed (1 Cor. 2:10) to the believer's spirit, which is of God (1 Cor. 2:12). Many may struggle with the temptation to compromise. However, not compromising requires our unswerving submission to God only. An eloquent, informative, persuasive presentation of the Word of God, absent revelation, draws the listener to reasoning rather than submission. We must be careful not to become so intrigued with witty speeches and conversations that we fall prey to compromise's partner in evil, deception.

"And this I say, lest any man should beguile [trick] you with enticing words. (5) For though I be absent in the flesh, yet am I with you in the spirit, joyful and beholding your order, and steadfastness of your faith in Christ. (6) As you have therefore received Christ Jesus the Lord, so walk ye in Him. (7) Rooted and built up in Him and established in the Faith as you have been taught, abounding therein with thanksgiving. (8) Beware lest any man spoil you through philosophy and vain deceit after the tradition of men, after the rudiments of the world, and not after Christ." Colossians 2:4-8 KJV

This text is derived from Paul's instructions to the church of Colosse and Laodicea. He had a sincere concern as it regarded the false doctrine they were receiving from Gnostics. Paul's words in Colossians two were a direct rebuttal to them. The Gnostics over-humanized Christ and openly resisted His commands. The Colossians were taught the right way; however, many considered the Gnostics' false messages, therefore forfeiting their benefits of the Cross. It is safe to assume that the enemy plans to deceive the people of God. We must become intentional about removing all disclaimers that we attempt to add to the Word of God. For instance, "He will keep me in perfect peace, but...", or He will never leave me nor forsake me, but...." Remember, God is Sovereign. He governs Himself. If He promises us that He will do it, our responsibility is to believe Him and not explain His process. When we humanize God, we give place to the devil to deceive. Once a person becomes deceived, it takes the Holy Spirit to awaken them from their deception. This, I say, "Deception is the road to compromise that leads to censorship. A church that will compromise is a church that can be silenced!"

Deception, the Road to Compromise

I have often pondered the process that the church goes through that eventually leads her to compromise. With an abundance of sound teaching that many of us have received during the span of our Christian walk with the Father, how do we conclude at doubting Him and compromising? We know that according to God's Word in Psalms 119:1-4, we ought not to compromise, but why do we? Furthermore, when we compromise, why is it so difficult to acknowledge as such? Satan has a powerful weapon called deception. He always launches it in stealth mode and is usually after a "God said."

Satan's purpose is to cause you to believe something that is not true to gain your worship. He detests God, but he is no match for God, so he targets what God loves the most, His church.

A biblical story immediately comes to mind when I think of this satanic device called deception. In 1 Kings 13, there is a story about "a man of God and the old Prophet." In a simple commentary, the man of God was instructed by the Lord for Jeroboam. The northern Kingdom of Israel has become amazingly comfortable with her new, false religion – the two golden calves. Jeroboam stands next to his altar offering incense to his false god when the man of God arrives, saying, "This is the sign which the Lord has spoken; Behold, the altar shall be rent, and the ashes that are upon it shall be poured out," (vs. 3). After speaking the Word of the Lord, the man of God instructions was to "eat no bread, nor drink water, nor turn again by the same way that he came" (vs. 9). Like many, the man of God started well. He did exactly as instructed until he was met by deception, disguised with a title.

"He (the old Prophet) said unto him, I am a Prophet also as you are; and an angel spoke unto me by the Word of the Lord, saying, Bring him back with you into your house, that he may eat bread and drink water. But he (the old prophet) lied unto him. So, he (the man of God) went back with him, and did eat bread in his house, and drank water." vs. 18-19

Look at how powerful deception is. The old prophet, who represents the apostate church, uses captivating verbiage in wooing the man of God into this satanic snare. The man of God's response was in direct disobedience to the instructions given to him by God. Inevitably, this would cost him his life.

"And when he (the man of God) was gone, a lion met him by the way, and slew him: and his carcass was cast in the way, and the ass stood by it, the lion also stood by the carcass." vs. 24

It may seem harsh of God to sentence a man to death because of disobedience. We must understand that the Love of God holds equality with the Judgement of God. Yes, He loves us. However, He remains Just. The greatest dangers that the church must become aware of are the "Jeroboams" and "the old Prophets" of our time. The "Jeroboams" are those that enter who represent the agenda and ways of the world. Meanwhile, the "old Prophets" represent those separated from the Will of the Lord. The cunning craftiness of these snares has one primary goal, to deceive. Once deceived, temptations to compromise are merciless and leaves one to believe that what they are doing is right in the sight of God. Scripture tells us that "there is a way that seems right unto a man, but the end thereof are the ways of death" (Prov. 14:12 KJV). Great works, religious dialogs, or deepened facial expressions are not indicative of an obedient servant. Jesus says, to His disciples, "Whoever has My commandments and keeps them, he it is who loves Me..." (John 14:21a ESV). The precise meaning of the passage is that obedience to Christ's commandments is both a sign and a test of our unwavering love for Him. There are ways in which we love to do things, but if it is not His way, and we insist on doing it our way, it will lead to spiritual death.

"Be not deceived; God is not mocked, for whatever one sows, that will he also reap. For the one who sows to his own flesh will from the flesh reap corruption, but the one who sows to the Spirit will from the Spirit reap eternal life." Galatians 6:7-8 ESV

Paul warns believers not to allow false teaching to move their faith. Isn't it funny how we can have "great faith" while in the presence of God, but as soon as tainted teaching has been deposited into our ear, we suddenly have "little-to-no faith?" When we substitute something else for the Truth, we become deceived, and God mocked, with compromise being just around the corner. So, what is the answer to deception? Trust exclusively in Christ and His finished work on the Cross. In other words, "sowing to the Spirit," where we reap eternal life.

We have spent some time talking about deception. The need to understand Satan's process is consequential in avoiding the snare of compromise. The church should not be ignorant of Satan's device. You may be wondering what the connection between compromising and the Omnipotent Presence of God is. The fact is, there is no correlation between the All-Powerful God and compromise. I believe, as the church, we forget the fact that we serve a Holy God. There is no sin in Him, and because compromising the Word of God is sin, we should not be ignorant of this vice in His church. We cannot profess to be holy and righteous yet live carnal lives. We must keep with the precepts of the scripture and not compromise our biblical beliefs by being similar to the world. When we do, we are allowing the things of the world and its sensual allurements to take precedence over the Word of God. The description that Jesus gives us is in Matthew 13:22, KJV.

"He also who receives seed among the thorns is he who hears the Word, and the care of this world, and the deceitfulness of riches, choke the Word, and he becomes unfruitful."

Much of the modern-day church has professed to believing God and submitting to God only. However, some compromise their faith by desiring worldly success and accolades from man. Jesus says in John 5:41-44 ESV, "How can you believe when you receive glory from one another and do not seek the Glory that comes from God?" To compromise in one's total allegiance and devotion to God is to allow the world and its accompanying worries to take precedence over the Word of God. When this happens, we exchange His righteousness for our self-righteousness, which hinders us from being in His presence.

"Take care, brothers, lest there be in any of you an evil, unbelieving heart, leading you to fall away from the living God." Hebrews 3:12 ESV

Desiring Presence over Recognition

Self-entitlement, self-centeredness, and self-indulgence present some of the most challenging fights for the church. I personally believe that it is easier to get a sinner saved than a saint delivered. Often, sinners are looking for answers. Meanwhile, there are portions of the church that believe "they are the answer." So, the church sometimes finds herself approaching God, all the while competing with His Presence for recognition. Compromising what we know about God for the sake of being recognized is extremely dangerous. God has graced His church with many talents, skills, and gifts. The temptation to self-focus must be renounced. This very thing is what caused Lucifer's ejection out of heaven.

"Your heart was lifted up because of your beauty; you have corrupted your wisdom by reason of your brightness: I will cast you to the ground, I will lay you before kings, that they may behold you." Ezekiel 28:17 KJV

Once again, Lucifer fell because of pride. He removed his eyes from the One Who sits on the throne, noticing his own beauty as it grew more and more in his own eyes. He was changed from "the anointed Cherub who covers" (vs. 14) to "the one whose heart was lifted up" (vs. 17). It is disheartening to know that the church, at times, will remove her eyes from the One Who anoints to herself. We will get engrossed with our beautiful sanctuaries and euphonious voices and bands that we will become intoxicated with the applauds of others. Sometimes, not noticing that the anointing has been removed. When recognition is desired over God's Presence, the tragedy of losing the anointing is without question.

We have seen this with Lucifer, but I remember a man by the name of King Saul. God chose him and sent him to Samuel so that Samuel could anoint him with oil and consecrate him as King (1 Sam. 9:15,16). Even though the Prophet Samuel did the anointing with the oil, the anointing is recognized as coming from the Lord (1 Sam. 15:17). Let us remain aware of this very thing; it is God's Omnipotent Presence on His gift that makes the difference. Saul was anointed for only two years. He was rejected as King and lost his anointing because he was disobedient to the Word of the Lord.

"Now go and smite Amalek, and utterly destroy all that they have, and spare them not; but slay both man and woman, infant and suckling, ox and sheep, camel and ass." 1 Samuel 15:3 KJV

"But Saul and the people spared Agag, and the best of the sheep, and of the oxen, and of the fatlings, and the Lambs, and all that was good, and would not utterly destroy them: but everything that was vile and refuse, that they destroyed utterly." 1 Samuel 15:9 KJV

Thus, we have a perfect picture of Saul's direct disobedience and self-centeredness, as well, of modern Christendom. God will only accept total obedience from His church and will reject self-willed and self-centeredness. With both Lucifer and Saul, attention was taken from God and place on themselves and their agenda. The Omnipotent Presence of God is awe-inspiring and should never have to compete with personal recognition. All that we are is because of the obedience of the Sacrificial Lamb to His Father. Learning to pattern our lives after the life of Jesus, we decrease the risk of being deceived by the enemy and falling into compromise. Compromise shows our lack of faith in God and, as the Word states, "And without faith, it is impossible to please God..." (Heb. 11:6 NIV). Impossible is a very strong word. Therefore, let it be noted that, without faith, the chance of pleasing God will not be able to occur, exist, or be done. With this being said, we will be the church that stands on the Word of God. We will not just hear it but obey it (Lk. 11:28) because we love the Lord (Jn. 14:15). Deception will not be the road that we travel that leads us to make concessions against the Word of God. God's church will not depend on our understanding, but His, and will be the end-time church of "No Compromise."

Can you sing with me?

My hope is built on nothing less
Than Jesus' blood and righteousness
I dare not trust the sweetest frame
But wholly lean on Jesus' name

On Christ the Solid Rock I stand
All other ground is sinking sand
All other ground is sinking sand
Amen!

5

THE
OMNIPOTENT
PRESENCE
G*of*OD

Fully Submitted to the Father

Being the youngest of thirteen children, and in my own opinion, getting my way most of the time, I remember telling my older siblings, "You can't tell me what to do...you ain't my daddy." As funny as it sounds today, this is the very attitude that we will take when submitting to authority. By the way, the word "submit" is not vulgar language. Still, when we hear the Word, something in us causes us to cringe. This world has been made to believe that you can do what you want to do. Although this might be true for them, this is not a belief in the Kingdom of God. We are all submitting to something and someone. Our responsibility as believers is to be sure that our submission is to God and His Word. The Omnipotent Presence of God requires our complete submission to Him. Recognizing that "He is our Father" should instantly bring us to the place of humility and submission. Others may yet be able to instruct you. Nevertheless, through the loving hand of God and the trying of our reins, He prepares our wounded hearts to submit to Him and others willingly.

"Examine Me, O Lord, and prove Me; try My reins and My heart." Psalms 26:2 KJV

As children of God, we should inquire of the Holy Spirit to probe deep within our hearts. Why? To affirm whether or not we are abiding in the Word of God. When God searches our hearts and finds the inability to submit is present, He will try our reins. This is simply Him allowing certain particulars to happen in our lives to surface those things that laid dormant, causing us to rebel. Let us remove our minds from what we want and think and submit ourselves to Him as obedient vessels.

"For the mind that is set on the flesh is hostile to God, for it does not submit to God's law; indeed, it cannot." 1 Peter 5:5 ESV

Biblical Submission

The word "submission" is defined through various sources as accepting or yielding to a superior entity or another person's authority or will. To stop trying to fight or resist something or someone; to agree to do or accept something you have been resisting or opposing. This definition gives some understanding, but let us look at Jesus as our example. Let us examine the relationship between Him and His Father.

"Who, being in the form of God, thought it not robbery to be equal with God. (7) But made Himself of no reputation, and took upon Him the form of a servant, and was made in the likeness of men. (8) And being found in fashion as a man, He humbled Himself and became obedient unto death, even the death of the Cross." Philippians 2:6-8 KJV

As disciples, the Word of God instructs us to "sit down first and count the cost..." (Luke 14:33 KJV). A misconception of salvation, particularly after being saved a while, is that we have now become someone to be noticed. Some even covet the spotlight and stage in hopes of building a brand or making a name for themselves (Gen. 11:4 KJV). Jesus does just the opposite. He made Himself of no reputation. Even though He was God in the flesh, He humbled Himself and submitted all authority to His Father. So, the question is, "Have we counted the cost?" Can we do the work of our heavenly Father and be submitted to Him, making ourselves of no reputation?

This book's title, "The Omnipotent Presence of God," points solely to the Holy Spirit-filled church. In the Person of the Holy Spirit, the all-powerful presence of God helps us submit to the Father. Without the Holy Spirit, total submission to God is impossible. Our flesh loves to "fill good." The works of the flesh (Gal. 5:19-21) anxiously await an opportunity to induce pleasure upon our bodies. For a Christian to walk in complete submission to the Father, being baptized by the Spirit is imperative.

"This, I say then, Walk in the Spirit, and you shall not fulfill the lust of the flesh. (17) For the flesh lusteth against the Spirit and the Spirit against the flesh, and these are contrary the one to the other

so that you cannot do the things that you would." Galatians 5:16-17 KJV

May I, for a moment, share a concern? With the lack of acknowledgment of the Holy Spirit in modern-day church and the rejecting of His Gifts, Character, and Language, I sense that the church has become mesmerized by all the lights, cameras, and fame. Some will be moved to respond by saying, "The dynamics of how we do church has evolved." It is unfortunate, but I sadly agree. We have evolved into a people who reject God's authority (Heb. 13:17) and preachers who refuse to preach that God demands us to be Holy (1 Pet. 1:16). So instead of "walking in the Spirit and not fulfilling the lust of the flesh," we will walk in our flesh, fulfilling lustful feelings that hinder us from submitting to the omnipotent presence of God. I get it. How I speak will not "pack the house." However, my charge and focus are not to pack the house but the Kingdom by feeding God's people with Knowledge and Understanding (Jer. 3:15 KJV). Consistency in submission to God and each other automatically closes the door to pride and the enemy. The Word of God says, "Submit yourselves therefore to God. Resist the devil, and he will flee from you" (James 4:7KJV). Attempting to resist the devil without first submitting yourself to God is a wasted effort. So here is the definition of biblical submission:

"He must increase, but I must decrease." John 3:30 KJV

Very simple, right? Jesus Christ must forever "increase" in our hearts. Not man, denominational beliefs, religious titles, or offices, but Jesus. Moreover, we must "decrease" by submitting and making ourselves of no reputation. To ministers of the

Gospel of Jesus Christ, I encourage you to regard Divine Authority and self-depletion as we prepare His Bride for His coming. We must hide behind the Greater Glory of our Lord. We are effective only as we succeed in submission. I hope that "the church," through total submission, will find her way back to the Word of God. The Apostle Paul says, "Those things, which you have both learned, and received, and heard, and seen in me, do" (Phil 4:9 KJV). Paul had preached the Gospel of Jesus Christ and lived righteously before them. The people witnessed the Gospel at work in him; therefore, he instructs them to do the same. A superb example that the church has today is still Jesus Christ. After all, He is the Word. I believe significant change could occur if the world could look at the church and see the Word rather than a reflection of themselves.

Yes, Lord, I will do it. Or will I?

"Now, therefore, if you will obey My Voice indeed, and keep My Covenant, then you shall be a Peculiar Treasure unto Me above all people: for all the earth is mine. (6) And you shall be unto me a kingdom of Priests and a Holy Nation. These are the words which you shall speak unto the children of Israel. (8) And all the people answered together, and said, All that the Lord has spoken, we will do...." Exodus 19:5,6 and 8

It is often said that some people listen to respond rather than listen to hear. Such a pithy observation, however, contains a general truth. We will hear the word of God being preached, all the while envisaging in our mind a self-beneficial, self-justifying response. This is why we can shout over a word given in church but leave the church offended and deny its applicability. In a parable, Jesus speaks of this, saying, "But he who receives the seed (Word of God) into stony places, the same is he who hears the Word and immediately with joy receives it. Yet has he not root in himself but endures for a while: for when tribulation or persecution arises because of the Word, by and by he is offended" (Matt. 13:20-21 KJV).

Let us be honest. Have you ever wondered why we will say "yes" to God when the Word is given but never walk in what He has said? The excuses we will give others who witnessed the moment are, "well, God has me resting," or "I am just waiting on the Lord," or "I am in a season of rest." Is it possible that we responded emotionally to the word but then became offended "when tribulation or persecution arose because of the Word?" In no way am I insinuating that waiting and resting in God is wrong. However, we use these phrases as a stalling tactic until we feel the time is right for us to obey. There are several places in scripture when God gives a promise. For us to receive the promise, we must first meet the conditions. Again, He says, "If you will obey My voice indeed, and keep My Covenant, then you shall be a Peculiar Treasure unto Me above all people...." The children of Israel had just gone forth out of the land of Egypt and into the wilderness of Sinai. Moses goes up the mountain to speak with God about the people. The first instruction given by God was to "obey My Voice." Total submission to God requires absolute obedience to His Voice. Since the beginning of time, we have claimed our ability to obey God, but given time, we have failed terribly in doing so. Had the children of Israel known their hearts' condition, they would have replied that such conditions would have been impossible for them to meet. In turn, they would have submitted themselves to God, giving Him the liberty to provide them with new hearts capable of obedience to His Voice. The key to submitting to God is knowing that the soil of our heart is ready to receive "seed" (Lk 8:11) and willing to have waste removed (Ps. 51:10). To say, "yes, Lord, I will do it," and genuinely mean it, you must first make an appointment with "The Cardiologist."

Spiritual Electrocardiogram

Because God is far wiser than man could ever be, it is appreciated when He gives revelation from practical moments. Because of my experience as a Combat Medic in the United States Army, God will, at times, speak to me through the limited knowledge I have of the human anatomy. I must say that my greater interest is in operation and function of the heart. So when He compares using the natural heart to explain or clarify the spiritual heart, it deepens my appreciation and gratitude for Who He truly Is. As a medic, I have learned that the human body contains five organs that are considered vital for survival. They are the heart, brain, kidneys, liver, and lungs. Whenever one organ malfunctions, the person is usually referred to a doctor specializing in that organ's function. In categorizing these in order of most importance, I would favor the heart if that is possible. Why? Because I am fascinated with its responsibilities. Naturally, a properly functioning heart sends oxygen and nutrients to all parts of the body along with hormones and other vital substances, giving it what it needs to function. Let me pause for a moment. I am not a doctor or nurse, and I have been away from my medical training for twenty-five years. However, if you are and you feel my assessment is incomplete, please give me some grace. As I was leading to say, the benefits a body receives from a healthy natural heart closely relate to having a healthy spiritual heart. As it pertains to this one particular organ, when healthy, the body lives.

Having heart problems can be a scary thing. By the grace of God, I do not speak from experience, but I do know others who do. There are constant visits to the heart specialist, the Cardiologist. The Cardiologist is a doctor who specializes in the study or treatment of heart diseases and heart abnormalities. To determine what condition your heart is in, he will order an electrocardiogram or EKG to be done on your heart. Usually, from the results of that examination, the Cardiologist will start treatment. How closely this relates to the spiritual heart. When the body is not functioning properly, and works of the flesh are alive (Gal. 5:19-21), or if there is an absence of the Fruit of the Spirit (Gal. 5:22-23), we need to see, "The Cardiologist." An old song says, "He is a heart fixer and a mind regulator." Yes, He Is, and He is the only One Who can fix a bad heart. We are talking about Jesus.

"The heart is deceitful above all things, and desperately wicked, who can know it? I the Lord search the heart, I try the reins, even to give every man according to his ways, and according to the fruit of his doing." Jeremiah 17:9-10 KJV

The Omniscient God knows the hopeless corruption in man's heart. This is why He allows certain things to happen in our lives to surface those things hidden in our hearts. In other words, "He tries the reins." Also, so man will not say that we were unjustly judged, God will make things happen or allow things to happen in our lives, which will always reveal precisely what is in our hearts. Those happenings or situations are what I call a "Spiritual Electrocardiogram." Have you ever heard a "cuss" word fly out of someone's mouth after slamming their finger or stubbing their toe? They will immediately say, "I am sorry, I do not know where that came from." Well, "The Cardiologist," our heavenly Father knew it was there, and the results from the "Spiritual Electrocardiogram," the slamming of the finger or stubbing of the toe, proved it. Now that you have seen the results, the Cardiologist will now give the treatment plan, REPENT!

I truly believe that the pandemic in the land is God's Spiritual EKG used to reveal the condition of the heart of His church. We had seen the results present in the church before the pandemic was allowed [notice, allowed, not caused]. The true "sons of God" are those the Holy Spirit leads (Rom. 8:14) to promote love, unity, prayer, and works that glorify God. On the other hand, illegitimate children (Heb. 12:8) are being led by the flesh (Rom. 8:5) to promote hatred, division, and works that glorify themselves. This spiritual EKG does not reveal to God what is in our hearts, for He already knows. Its purpose is to reveal to us what is in our hearts. Furthermore, the remedy is repentance! Rioting, protesting, marching, canceled culture or having racial reconciliation meetings WILL NOT REPLACE GOD'S PRESCRIPTION FOR SIN THAT WAS PURCHASED ON THE CROSS.

"I TELL YOU, NO, BUT, EXCEPT YOU REPENT, YOU SHALL ALL LIKEWISE PERISH" Luke 13:5

This prophetic utterance given to us through His Word should persuade repentance. If you are a child of God, but fear has open the door to anger, bitterness, retaliation, and the inability to submit to the Word of God, my question to you is this, "who put that in your heart?" Remember, the vision of Satan's kingdom is to steal, kill, and destroy (Jn. 10:10). His tactics to carry out his vision are through the lust of the flesh, the lust of the eyes, and the pride of life (1 Jn. 2:16). This very thing is exemplified in one of the disciples of Jesus, named Judas.

"Then, one of the Twelve, the one called Judas Iscariot, went to the chief priests and asked, "what are you willing to give me if I deliver Him over to you?" So they counted out for him thirty pieces of silver." Matthew 26:14-15 NIV

Judas's request to the chief priest was extremely disturbing. He requested payment to double-cross Jesus, fulfilling the lust of his flesh. Who, in their right mind, would do such a thing? I will tell you how this thing happened.

"And supper being ended, the devil having now put into the heart of Judas Iscariot, Simon's son, to betray Jesus." John 13:2 KJV

The corrupted heart of Judas causes him to betray Jesus. His heart was filled with betrayal because the devil put it there. So again, my question to you is, "who put the anger, fear, retaliation, and the inability to submit to the Word of God in your heart? What was your price?" Listen, people of God, allow God to fix your heart and remove the waste that's been deposited by the devil and repent. The Word of God says,

"There is a way that seems right to man, but its end is the way of death (Prov. 14:12)." There is an All-Powerful Presence of God that's perceptible by touch. Reach out to Him and allow Him to heal you. This is the only way that you can become fully submitted to Him. Not our way, His way!

Left blank intentionally.

6

THE OMNIPOTENT PRESENCE GOD *of*

An All-Powerful Presence

I have yearned for inspiration and revelation from the Holy Spirit to write this chapter. The time could not come quick enough. As I begin to write, I feel an anointing much different from that of the previous chapters. My truth is this; I want more of God. I want to experience the God of the Bible. In my search for more, I often reminisce about past life experiences. The peace gained from experiencing the nearness of my Heavenly Father took me to desire to need His Presence. God's method for His Presence is simple, He says, "Then you shall call upon Me, and you shall go and pray unto Me, and I will hearken unto You. And ye shall seek Me, and find Me when ye shall search for Me with all your heart," (Jer. 29:12-13 KJV). Some of the lessons I have learned came from experiences that contradicted scripture. Those experiences impelled me into studying the Word for myself and searching for God with all my heart. When I began pastoring, a great Word of Wisdom given to me was, "you MUST have a prayer life." Now prayer is my life, and it was in prayer that He revealed to me His All-Powerful Presence. His Presence should be palpable in our prayer time, our works, and our worship. If not, pray this prayer, "Create in me a clean heart, O God, and renew a right spirit within me. Cast me not away from thy presence and take not thy Holy Spirit from me" (Ps. 51:10-11 KJV). A significant hindrance to Presence is usually found in the heart of self. If you find yourself in a place where you are not experiencing His Presence, look deep inside yourself and see if you are trying to control how He presents Himself to you.

Presence in Prayer

Funny story. I remember being asked by a deacon of a church I visited to do the invocation. Though answering yes, I was completely confused as to what was being asked of me. So I did what any Holy Ghost-filled pastor would do; I googled, "what is an invocation in a traditional Baptist church?" The answer did not satisfy my concern, and I began to feel a slight panic. I cannot possibly stand before all these people and preachers and pray how I usually pray, I thought. I knew that if my responsibility was to request God's Presence, I would eventually end up interceding and spiritually warring for the people. For the time I was there, I was reminded of 1 Corinthians 1:29, "That no flesh shall glory in His Presence." I knew that because flesh was very active in the house, the Presence of God was needed. So, through the Holy Spirit, I prayed accordingly.

"Likewise, the Spirit also helps our infirmities, for we know not what we should pray for as we ought; but the Spirit Himself makes intercession for us with groanings which cannot be uttered." Romans 8:26 KJV

One of the greatest weapons of warfare given to the believer is prayer. Prayer is the area in our lives where Satan fights us the most and wages war against our time. He knows that if he can fill our time with things we want to do, we will not have the intimacy with our Father that He desires. Prayer is not a moment of meditation or passive reflection; it is communication with our Father. A saying in the church is that "when it comes to prayer, it is not how long you pray, it is the quality of prayer." This sounds good and obtains some truth but has the danger of being misleading. If prayer is a dialog between God and the believer, to include fellowship with God, what if He wants to speak, but we do not have the time? How many times have you gone to a person with a concern, but they did all the talking, and when it was your turn to speak, they had to depart? How did it make you feel? We must become intentional about praying. My heart grieves to know that many believers and church leaders do not like to pray. According to scripture, I have learned that this occurs because of an absence of humility (2 Chron. 7:14). When we are unwilling to exemplify a low estimate of ourselves before God, we lose our zeal for prayer. Humility is the key to having a healthy prayer life. There will be moments when we will go into prayer but not sure of what to say. This is one of the purposes of the Holy Spirit. He prays in us the perfect will of God for our lives.

"And He Who searches the hearts knows what is the Mind of the Spirit because He makes intercession for the Saints according to the Will of God." Romans 8:27 KJV

Understanding that the Holy Spirit prays within us validates His Presence and as well, the importance of being filled with the Holy Spirit. Our Heavenly Father looks within our hearts to see the Mind of the Spirit and the intercession made on our behalf. The single and most important goal of the Holy Spirit is to carry out the perfect and divine Will of the Father in our lives. In being our Comforter, we can still have peace without knowing His exact plan. He not only comforts us, but He helps carry out God's plan in our lives.

When we pray to God, there is no other conversation on earth that can compare. When you mature in your prayer life, you will begin to understand that He has just as much to say to you as you to Him. However, this is not to say that our petitions are not important to Him. Paul wrote, "Do not be anxious about anything, but in every situation, by prayer and petition, with thanksgiving, present your requests to God" (Phil. 4:6 ESV). Remember this, whether you are asking or listening, when a believer prays, things happen. We know this as the "power of prayer." This Power comes solely from the Omnipotent God. It does not flow from us; it is not found in how we pray or the use of eloquent verbiage. The Power of prayer does not come from soft music, dramatic voice level changes, or dimmed lights. This Power emerges from God to Whom we pray. He is the source of all Power. Because of prayer, we can experience the Omnipotent Presence of God.

"These all continued with one accord in prayer and supplication, with women, and Mary the Mother of Jesus, and with His brethren." Acts. 1:14 KJV

"And when the Day of Pentecost was fully come, they were all with one accord in one place. And suddenly there came a sound from Heaven as of a mighty rushing wind, and it filled all the house where they were sitting. And there appeared unto them cloven tongues like fire, and it sat upon each of them. And they were all filled with the Holy Spirit and began to speak with other tongues, as the Spirit gave them utterance." Acts 2:1-4 KJV

We will now transition from our prayer time to corporate prayer. Can you imagine what God would do if believers could come together on one accord and pray? It sounds horrible to use the words "believer" and "pray" in the same sentence, with them opposing each other. A universal problem in the church today is getting "believers" to attend corporate prayer. Why is corporate prayer so unimportant to some "believers and leaders?" The answer is relatively simple but rarely accepted.

"Those who live according to the flesh have their minds set on what the flesh desires, but those who live in accordance with the Spirit have their minds set on what the Spirit desires." Romans 8:5 NIV

As I write, I cannot help but think of how hard the enemy is fighting God's leaders in keeping the church doors closed. At the same time, I am appalled at how many have given in to his attacks. With a preponderance of reasons given in hopes to justify doing so, many leaders leaned to their understanding just in case God is not Whom He says He is. The repercussions in doing so hindered much-needed Acts chapter two experiences. Thank God for the remnants throughout the Body of Christ, who continually join on one accord requesting the Omnipotent Presence of God.

By using Acts chapter two as a means to understand God's Presence in prayer, we gain knowledge through the definition of the word "accord." Accord is "being in harmony or agreement with." Those who were present in the upper room, an estimated total of about 120 (Acts 2:8) to include the Apostles, were in agreement as to why they were there. This very act of harmony prompted an immediate response from Heaven. Did they experience Presence because of Peter's excellent teaching, or how well they prayed? The answer to both is an emphatic "No." They experienced the Presence of God because they were all on one accord with an expectation of Presence.

"Now I beseech you, brethren, by the name of our Lord Jesus Christ that you all speak the same thing, and that there be no divisions among you, but that you be perfectly joined together in the same mind and in the same judgment." 1 Corinthians 1:10 KJV

The implication in this verse demands unity concerning the Person Jesus Christ. How awesome it would be if the Body of Christ developed prayer sessions out of a passion for Jesus rather than an intricate demonstration of religious ritual. Wanting to pray and agree with others in prayer should be the moral and spiritual qualities distinctive to the church. After all, should we anticipate God's Presence if He is not truly wanted?

Presence in Our Work

In the New Testament alone, when Jesus arrived on the scene, miracles, signs, and wonders happened often. Blind men were healed (Mat. 9:27-31), dumb spirits were cast out (Mat. 9:32-33). A widow's son rose to life at Nain (Lk. 7:11-17), and ten lepers were cleansed (Lk. 17:11-19). Lazarus was raised from the dead at Bethany (Jn. 11:38-44). Demonic in the synagogue healed (Mk. 1:23). Peter's mother-in-law healed (Mat. 8:14), and the tempest stilled (Mat 8:23). A paralytic healed (Mat. 9:2), and an uncleaned spirit was cast out (Mat. 17:14). Shall I go on? These things happened when Jesus arrived on the scene. Very different from what is happening today. Jesus speaks to His disciples, saying:

"Verily, verily, I say unto you, He who believes on Me, the Works that I do shall he do also; and greater works than these shall he do because I go unto My Father." John 14:12 KJV

Believing in Jesus Christ and the finished work on the Cross gives the believer power, through the Holy Spirit, to do the works. The narrative given is not at all referring to quality but quantity. The works of Jesus were confined to greater Israel, while the believer's works cover the entire world. If this be the case, and it is, we should be experiencing these same miracles, signs, and wonders today. Why? Because Jesus Who once walked alongside us (Jn 1:14) now lives in us (Jn 14:23). As the church, we have mastered how to create an environment to have "good church" but failed terribly in creating an atmosphere worthy of "His Omnipotent Presence." It may never be admitted, but for many leaders today, the way Jesus functions does not fit into their plans on "growing their church in numbers." They have justified their fear of "Presence" by redefining the Holy Spirit's responsibilities.

For this reason, many are sick, spiritually, and mentally bound in the church today. They have fired the "Great Physician" and rely on medical interns (those unskilled in spiritual things) to bring in a new methodology that will keep God's people present but afflicted. It is time, to be honest and face a dreadful truth. The pastor's salary, church building, sound equipment, lights, and staff are significant financial burdens and concerns to a leader. All that is mentioned cannot be financially satisfied if there are no people inside the four walls. Because the time has come when people will not endure sound doctrine (2 Tim. 4:3), some leaders feel the enormous pressure that if they preach the message of the Kingdom of God, where a Sovereign God rules, they will lose the people. So they become teachers who will satisfy the itching ear of the people, creating a people driven by emotion that's absent of Presence. The message should be clear by now; we need the Holy Spirit. We need His All-Powerful Presence, not to demonstrate a religious performance but to carry out, accomplish, and fulfill God's work.

There is a deliberate display of humility in those who recognize that God chooses such unworthy vessels to carry out His work on earth.

"But the Lord said unto me, Say not, I am a child, for you shall go to all that I shall send you, and whatsoever I command you, you shall speak. Be not afraid of their faces, for I am with you to deliver you, saith the Lord." Jeremiah 1:7-8

Almost immediately upon God's commands, the flesh withdraws and becomes susceptible to fear, lacking in faith. This was the case with Jeremiah and Moses, Jonah, Elijah, and a few others. The call of God greatly demands absolute obedience that coincides with absolute submission and humility. The desire for many is that God would enlarge their territory, and so should it be. However, Peter says this, "Humble yourselves therefore under the Mighty Hand of God, that He may exalt you in due time" (1 Pet. 5:6 KJV). Recognizing one's unworthiness in the Presence of the All-Powerful God satisfies the divine condition for elevation. God's exaltation of a believer is never done to prove how great we are, but for His Glory, which emerges from the believer's character.

We all endeavor to invite God's Presence into our work. We understand that doing so releases His favor and brings into being a firm foundation for the work that's being done.

"Let the favor of the Lord our God be upon us and establish the work of our hands upon us; yes, establish the work of our hands." Psalms 90:17 ESV

It is incredibly refreshing to experience a move of God in a service. It is undoubtedly recognized that the work that went into it was sanctioned by God and favored by Him. Feelings of gratitude and thanksgiving saturate the atmosphere. His Presence fills the place, releasing salvation to the lost, restoring the broken, and deliverance to the bound. Adoration begins to trickle from the mouths of those in the Spirit, inevitably leading to an outpour of worship. All because He was considered and invited in the work. I would be remised in avoiding this statement. No matter the size of the gathering, or the significance of your work to others, if God's hand is on it, His Presence will be in it. God, Himself will be our courage, power, and strength. He says to Israel and us, "For I the Lord your God will hold your right hand, saying unto you, fear not, I will help you (Is. 41:13 KJV)." The Word of the Lord has spoken. Now go forth, child of God, "be careful to obey all the commands of the Lord your God, following His instructions in every detail (Deut. 5:32 NIV)."

Presence in Worship

Great displeasure experienced as a believer came when I discovered that praise and worship were not the same. My ignorance of the fact transpired from years of erroneous teaching and many religious, corporate experiences. As I matured in God, I began to realize that something had to be missing. The truth of true worship came to me during a time when I desperately needed God. I was in a season where I was about to give up. I had asked God over and over again to remove the enormous pain that encumbered me. However, it felt as if He extended the time rather than shortening it. To my dismay, the required class in the life of a worshipper had just commenced. I remember being told by the Holy Spirit that I needed to accept the Father's plan for my life and repent for not doing so. While tears flowed from my eyes and immense pain increased from my heart, I whispered to my Father, "I accept your plan...please forgive me." In all honesty, the fact that I accepted God's plan for my life brought no understanding of that plan. I was utterly oblivious to what I should do next. A short time later, the Holy Spirit began to train me in how to worship a King. He revealed my identity as a priest (1 Pet. 2:9) of a Mighty King, God the Father who truly loved me. I felt compassion by being with Him. The Holy Spirit prompted me to begin thanking Him for all He has done for and in me (Ps. 100:4). Although I had a relationship with God before this particular season, the intense intimacy gained when becoming a worshipper developed a oneness with my Heavenly Father that immediately triggered growth.

"In everything, give thanks, for this is the Will of God in Christ Jesus concerning you." 1 Thessalonians 5:18

Experiencing the Presence of God in worship, one must have a heart of thanksgiving. An initial lesson learned as a worshipper is that, although worship acknowledges the Father for Who He Is, praise is thanking Him for all He has done. No matter the outcome of a situation or how negative things may appear, we are never to cease thanking the Lord, for this is the Will of God. The relevance for maturing is shown here. The statement of giving thanks in 1 Thessalonians 5:18 is not merely a suggestion but a command. Mature believers understand that if we love God, we are to keep His commandments (Jn 14:15). A heart of gratitude and thanksgiving becomes the vehicle that will usher you into the Presence of the Father. The temptation to complain is always lurking and never-ending. Still, thanksgiving to God is a privilege to the one who believes and trusts in Him.

We can quickly become engrossed with our personal needs when we pray and fascinated with blessings when we praise. However, when we worship God, nothing else matters. The beauty of authentic and genuine worship is that it is all about our Heavenly Father. A great misconception in today's church is that worship is "a thing" demonstrated by a person or people to induce high levels of emotion. For instance, we have been deceived in our thinking that worship is a type of music. In receiving this mistaken impression, we will form an opinion about worship based on our approval or disapproval of the music. If we disapprove of the type of music, then we cannot worship. Although applicable in some instances, this description cannot be relied on as truth. The problem is this, if worship was music only, then it was made for people and not for God. If worship is for people, then people are the object of worship and become gods to themselves. It benefits us to know that music, like praise, is intended to carry us into His Presence and not the spotlight. The tool of music that's given to us by God moves our body, soul, and spirit. An example of this is given to us in the book of Samuel.

"And it came to pass, when the evil spirit from God was upon Saul, that David took a harp, and played with his hands, so Saul was refreshed, and was well, and the evil spirit departed from him." 1 Samuel 16:23

Our spirits were created to respond to music. This is an incredible gift from God. However, it is not worship.

So what is worship? Worship is a compressed form of the Old English term "worth-ship," which means giving something or someone worth. It is done by demonstratively attributing value to that person or thing. In other words, we worship God by communicating and demonstrating His value. When we, as believers, show value to God, there is a tremendous cost. This is why worship is often associated with sacrifice. We make ourselves a sacrifice for Him because His value is so precious that it cannot be determined.

"I appeal to you, therefore brothers, by the mercies of God, to present your bodies as a living sacrifice, holy and acceptable to God, which is your spiritual worship." Romans 12:1 ESV

In addition to music, it is also assumed that worship is lifting our hands, speaking in unknown tongues, or bowing before Him. Although these may manifest in a person who worships, again, these actions are not worship. Let us look at it this way. If you examine a marathon runner's performance, you will witness speed, strength, endurance, and fatigue resistance abilities. It is not accurate to assume that these people just got out of bed one morning and went out and won a race. In the articles I have read about marathon runners, all information points to the fact that a successful marathon runner lives a sacrificed-filled life. They have strict eating and sleeping habits. They must maintain a proper weight in conjunction with being physically and mentally fit. In other words, a runner's actions that we see in a race come from a sacrificial life of a runner that's lived. As it pertains to worship, the lifting of our hands unto the Lord and speaking in an unknown tongue flow out of a sacrificial and consecrated body that is holy and acceptable to God. If you still missed it, here, you go. Worship is the life that we live that has been accepted by God to be holy and righteous and obedient to His Word. Worship comes from the spirit of a person who knows the Father (Jn. 4:22 and 24). Anyone can tell God thank you, but a true worshipper's holy lifestyle is their spiritual worship.

Left blank intentionally.

THE
OMNIPOTENT
PRESENCE
G *of* OD

Conclusion

With enormous pain and suffering throughout this world and the church, the message is clear. We need a powerful presence of God and not just a visitation. We need to see and experience the supernatural. He is known to be in a class all by Himself. No one is greater than He, in the heavens or the earth. He does the impossible. He embodies the believer as the same All-Powerful God, and His Will is for His church to exemplify this Power. The church has operated decades in mediocrity, commonplaceness, and ordinariness. She has not had the quality of being different, unexpected, or unique in any way. Sheep come into her sick and leave sick. They come into her bound, and they leave bound. She has become a sanctuary of comfortability rather than God's kingdom of Character. The world knows her as the newest up-and-coming partner in the entertainment industry, driven by a desire to be popular. Praise be to our God. He has raised up "sons," empowered by His Spirit to prepare His sheep for His Son's return. He has commissioned them as His agents to "go into all the world and preach the Gospel to every creature…and these signs shall follow them who believe, in My Name shall they cast out devils, they shall speak with new tongues. They shall put away serpents, and if they drink any deadly thing, it shall not hurt them; they shall lay hands on the sick. They shall recover, (Mk. 16:15,17-18 KJV)." The year of 2020 was the year of labor induction into the birth of these "sons" of God. That year brought some physical, emotional and financial sufferings that produced perseverance, character, and hope (Rom. 5:3-4). A picture of God's empowered church is appearing in the lives of His people. Miracles, signs, and wonders follow them because they believe in God. She is now becoming God's church who embraces His Presence, seeks His heart and will, never compromises, and is submitted to Him. Now the Truth of the Gospel will be preached, and lost souls will be saved. The sick will be healed, the bound delivered, and the wayward children will come home. All this is happening now because of the "Omnipotent Presence of God."

Left blank intentionally.

Left blank intentionally.

Made in the USA
Columbia, SC
21 December 2022

74151167R00046